MW01251695

Three Women of Hope

Three Women of Hope

Miriam, Hannah, Huldah

CHRISTIANNE MÉROZ

Translated by
DENNIS WIENK

WIPF & STOCK · Eugene, Oregon

Contents

Acknowledgments | vii

Prologue: Women who are Prophets Too | 1

1 Miriam the Nomad | 6

2 Hannah the Visionary | 27

3 Huldah the Townswoman | 46

Epilogue: Three Women of Hope | 56

Acknowledgments

Two words of thanks. First I wish to record here my thanks to Brother Pierre Schilling of the Monastery of the Epiphany, Eygalières, France, for his permission to use some of his ideas about Hannah's experience in the sanctuary of Shiloh.

I also want to thank all the women in the groups I facilitate at Woudsend, the Netherlands, who have enriched my reflection with their observations and discoveries as well as with their questions.

Women Who Are Prophets Too

THE LAND OF ISRAEL and its history are intimately connected with the prophets, and the hills and countryside of Judea are especially evocative of their presence. Even today you can see it in places like Ramah, Gibeah, and Anathoth. And Samuel has given his name to a long street in Jerusalem.

But what about the prophets who were women? Who remembers that two gates of the temple bore the name of the prophet Huldah, a woman? Some say that none of the holy books of the Abrahamic faiths—the Quran, the Bible, the Gospels, the Talmud—speak of prophets who were women, but this is a mistaken notion. The fact that we possess not a single scriptural book known to have been written by a woman can explain such an error, although it cannot excuse it. In fact the Bible presents us with numerous women prophets, in both Testaments. The Talmud, a collection of rabbinic writings, names seven of them in the First Testament—Sarah, Miriam, Deborah, Hannah, Abigail, Huldah, and Esther.

From among these women I have chosen to write about Miriam, Hannah, and Huldah—three women who

1

lived at crucial moments in the history of the Hebrew people. In very different contexts, they help us to discover a number of paths of liberation— liberation from slavery in Egypt and from despising the other, liberation from the prison of patriarchal structures, and liberation from a fascination with idols.

Centuries after these women lived their lives, we cannot shirk the questions about how oppressive situations like these are still the daily experience of women and men and children all over the world; hence the relevance of these women, all three of them, who learned how to be, and remain for us today, sources of hope.

A Word for Women and for Men

A well–known midrash claims that what Ezekiel saw in the sky one day (Ezek 1:1) is nothing compared with what the entire Hebrew people saw on the earth at the Red Sea one day. Ezekiel, and the other prophets too of course, did not see God; they only had visions of images of God. Someone has said that they were like people who meet up with an earthly king in the midst of his court and have to ask which one is the king. In utter contrast, at the crossing of the Red Sea the Israelites had no need to ask who the King was. As soon as they saw what was taking place, they all recognized him and said, "This is my God, and I will praise him" (Exod 15:2). Even ordinary folks at the Red Sea saw what Isaiah, Ezekiel, and the other prophets never saw.

After this founding event the whole people gather at the foot of Sinai, and God asks Moses to speak to the "house of Jacob" and to the "Israelites" (Exod 19:3; literally, "sons of Israel"). Why these two categories? Often we think they are equivalent expressions, but in the Bible a twofold expression like this is not mere repetition. Rashi, the noted

Jewish commentator of the eleventh century, gives as his explanation that the term "house of Jacob" represents the women whereas the term "Israelites" (literally, "sons of Israel") designates the men.

These men and these women form the "six hundred thousand souls" who, given their own lights, have heard and understood the words of God according to the Kabbalah, the medieval mystical commentary on Torah.

Giving Voice to the Silent Half

However, if each man, each woman has truly heard and understood, only the men have put the message into writing and rendered it visible. We therefore possess only "half of Torah," as Judith Plaskow, Professor of Religious Studies at Manhattan College in New York, puts it.

This fact shows that the founding experience of the Covenant at Sinai marks the beginning of the marginalization of woman (see Exod 19:15). If "all the people answered with one voice and said, 'All that the Lord has spoken we will do'" (Exod 24:3, 7), the fact is that Israel became thereby a male community in which the sign of the Covenant was thought to be only for the men.

Woman was not completely absent, but we meet her most often as the object of purity laws or as a metaphor describing the relationship between the people and God. Depending on the circumstances, some of the images for that relationship will be positive (beloved, sister) and others negative and devaluing (whore, harlot).

All interested women are hereby invited to become archeologists of the biblical texts in order to uncover their sisters, buried under the age-old weight of silence. To listen to them carefully and then give them back a face and voice, this is the task of our day. It is a task that is both fascinating and delicate. Then, alongside the great masculine themes that fill Scripture—war, government, organized worship—we will be able to add a feminine understanding and so give voice to the silent half of the Bible.

When Faithfulness Is Transformed into Adventure

To say who God is for a woman is the challenge. Renowned theologian Elisabeth Schüssler-Fiorenza, the Krister Stendahl Professor of Divinity at Harvard University, proposes a twofold interpretative key: a hermeneutics of suspicion and the recovery of an authentic remembered past. The first involves distrust of a tradition that has not known how, and has not wanted, to transmit the experience of women. The second involves memory of the past not in order to lament lost opportunities, but memory of the past that comes through hearing what the Spirit recalls to us.

Women have already been exhumed from their silence, and we are discovering that they have been able to put the powers that be in check, or at least destabilize them. Think of Tamar, Esther, and many others who, in the "white of Torah" (i.e., between the lines of Torah), on their own silent pathways, have written an entirely other history, which we are only beginning to uncover.

Miriam, Hannah, and Huldah are members of this group for whom the love of God and of his word is transformed into an adventure. They lived intensely, sometimes dangerously. Women with brains and hearts, these three prophets have seduced me.

My aim has not been to write a learned treatise on prophecy, and so I take a certain liberty in presenting these three lives. I propose simply to tell their stories and share my thoughts. After having listened to them closely myself,

I wanted to let them live for others with all their poetry, psychology, and theology . . .

1

Miriam the Nomad

MIRIAM COMES ONTO THE stage in the first chapters of the book of Exodus (2:1–10) at the time when the Hebrews are slaves in Egypt dealing with the shock of the decree Pharaoh has issued demanding the death of all the newborn Hebrew boys in the realm.

When the women, whose vocation after all is to safeguard life, were confronted with this plan of extermination, they immediately put a defensive strategy into place. Thanks to the Hebrew midwives, who courageously defied Pharaoh's order, their sons were shielded from death (1:17–20).

It is their creative disobedience that permits Miriam to enter salvation history through the act of saving her younger brother Moses from certain death.

1. THE SAVING ACT

Miriam is one of the seven prophets recognized by the Talmud who are women. She is therefore a member of that group of women and men whose role it is to look beyond and through events in order to announce something new, for that is the work of a prophet. The premises of this new thing are found hidden within the events themselves. The prophet's task is both to look into the future and to speak about it, since it is usually by means of the spoken word that prophets intervene in the course of history.

Seeing beyond Events

While prophets are noted for their visionary and interpretative gifts, they also stand out by their often nonconformist behavior. With a religious sensitivity ahead of their time, they are not afraid of critiquing cultural formalism. Defending the poor, making common cause with the rejected, they are themselves most often on the margins of society right alongside foreigners, women, widows, and orphans, alongside all those left behind. Prophets, both women and men, take on the role of intermediary between the divine and the human. They represent God to the world and the world to God.

In Jewish tradition it is usual to compare a prophet, again whether male or female, to a midwife. Just as the midwife sees the child who is coming into the world, the prophet sees what is going to happen. A midrash—traditional rabbinic commentary—illustrates this idea by making the midwives Shiphrah and Puah (Exod 1:15) the mother and another sister of Moses.

As she catches a glimpse of what is to happen, Miriam is one of those women who dared to defy Pharaoh (1:17), and, with Moses and Aaron, one of the three guides who were charged with leading their people from slavery in Egypt to freedom in the Promised Land (Mic 6:4).

A Messianic Calling

The story of Moses' rescue shows us how Miriam acted in her role as a prophet (Exod 2:4, 7). But before looking at it in detail, we pause at the beginning of that chapter in Exodus where there is a statement that seems to contradict what follows. A man from the house of Levi, we are told, took a daughter of Levi as his wife. She gave him a son (2:1). Later on we note that this child's sister hides in the bulrushes on the bank of the Nile in order to watch over her little brother.

So this "man from the house of Levi" is already father of a daughter. He is a married man. On this point the midrash offers a subtle explanation. It tells us that this representative of the tribe of Levi, after Pharaoh's decree condemning all newborn males to death (1:22), plans to separate from his wife so as no longer to procreate. But when little Miriam learns of it, she reminds her father that such a decision would make him complicit in the ruler's deadly policy, for not only would no more boys be born, but there would also be no more girls. The father recognizes his daughter's well-founded argument, and he decides to resume living with his wife. That is why, as the text tells us, he went to take a daughter of Levi as wife. The midrash adds that Miriam, who is five years old, and her brother Aaron, who is three, both danced at the time of their parents' remarriage. And to drive home the idea that Miriam was not just an ordinary girl, we are told that she made an announcement at the wedding feast that a son would be born and that he would be the savior of Israel. In legendary and poetic form this midrash lets us catch sight of how Miriam's vocation is both prophetic and messianic.

The child announced is in fact born. He is both handsome and good—the Hebrew adjective which describes him has the two meanings and is the same word that God uses to describe the results of the successive days of creation (Exod 2:2; cf. Gen 1:31).

For the first months the family manages to hide Moses and keep him from being killed. However, the more he grows, the greater the risk that he will be discovered, which would involve the condemnation of the whole family. So Miriam resolves to entrust his fate to the waters of the Nile. Placed in a reed basket, he will be discovered by Pharaoh's daughter and rescued from the water. The Hebrew word here for basket is the same as that used for the ark that Noah built.

It is at this moment that Miriam makes a decisive intervention. Before going any further however, we should point out that in this entire chapter the women, although they play such a determining role for the future of the savior of Israel, are completely anonymous. None of them has a name. They are all introduced simply in their roles as wife, sister, or daughter. Miriam herself is only the sister of Moses. This is a powerful reminder to attend to the matter of seeing to it that both a face and a name are given to all the women today who, at the peril of their lives, still fight against the forces of death and, more often than not, remain anonymous.

Looking from a Distance

Hidden in the bulrushes along the bank of the Nile, Miriam observes from afar what happens to her brother. She is not driven by simple curiosity, but, according to the midrash, by a pressing inner need to verify if what she announced at her parents' wedding has any chance of actually happening.

Behaving like the prophet she is, Miriam concentrates all her attention on her questioning and even more on what this questioning is going to become as it meets reality. She has predicted an exceptional future for her brother. She has seen the unseen. Now she must listen to what she has come to see.

In order to discern the divine and creative word in the unseen, Miriam stands at a distance (Exod 2:4). She not only keeps at a physical distance but also makes a kind of inner retreat from events as they unfold before her eyes. She must keep her eyes fixed both on the little basket as it keeps afloat on the water and on the future of this little child in danger, in whom she has seen the savior of Israel.

Miriam has understood that her brother's birth is not an ordinary event. From her entirely personal but very deep certainty she derives the strength to get through the suffering that abandoning the new baby means for her and the whole family. So she is completely clear-headed when she agrees to the adoption of the child by Pharaoh's daughter, and even suggests her own mother as nurse.

In the face of all these happy coincidences we might well wonder if mother and daughter were in league. Hebrew women are never short of strategies when it comes to saving their progeny. In addition, this complicity of mother and daughter, with which a third woman, Pharaoh's daughter, is associated, puts a bit of humanity into the otherwise dark episode of the death sentence for all male newborns.

Jewish exegesis takes note of the term that describes Miriam's attitude on the bank of the Nile: "his sister stood" (2:4), the narrative says, and this is akin to the same expression that is used to speak of the presence of God. For example, in the books of Samuel we read: "the Lord came and stood" (1 Sam 3:10). Miriam is not alone then on the bank of the Nile. The verb suggests that the divine presence lives in the girl. The Spirit is at work in her, and the divine presence, as the Hebrew notion would have it, already casts its shadow over the future savior of Israel.

The story of "Moses in the bulrushes" needs at least three ingredients: Pharaoh's decree, the Nile and its hospitable banks, and the initiative of courageous women. But to make a unique and marvelous narrative out of this drama, it also needs Miriam, the older sister who was bold enough to entrust her brother to the daughter of Pharaoh.

With a Stranger's Help

As soon as Pharaoh's daughter discovers the child, she recognizes that it is a little Hebrew boy whom someone is trying to protect from death. The narrative stresses that "she took pity" on this baby of only a few months. Perhaps she had the intuition of being part of something special. Did she have any inkling of the divine presence? The text remains silent on that score, and we know only that she made no objection to Miriam's proposal to find him a nurse.

In its simplicity her response to the girl: "Go" (Exod 2:8; KJV) reminds us of the account in Genesis where God calls Abraham: "Go from your country" (Gen 12:1). In the two texts we find the same verb, which, according to Rashi, can mean "follow your vocation." It is indeed a question of a geographical move—go find a nurse—but more existentially, of a move with respect to oneself, of setting out to weave one's particular vocation into the fabric of history.

Would Pharaoh's daughter also be a prophet when she goes against her father's decree? By sending Miriam to bring her project of rescuing her brother to a successful conclusion, she is participating in the reestablishment of justice. Her way of responding suggests just such a hypothesis, and it agrees well with the prophetic light with which the beginning of the chapter (Exod 2) is bathed. Like a bird, "a wind from God swept over the face of the waters" (Gen 1:2), this time the waters of the Nile, when the two women meet and combine their efforts and imagination in order to save the child.

Two Cultures for a Future Liberator

The exceptional circumstances of his childhood will allow Moses to participate in two different cultures. By his mother, now his nurse, he will be raised in the tradition of his people. By the daughter of Pharaoh, probably the daughter of Amenophis IV–Akhenaten, he will grow up in a free environment, sheltered from the sufferings and humiliations of slavery.

By giving two mothers to Moses, Miriam also gives him two cultures, and this will prepare him for his future responsibilities at the head of his people. His second birth, his birth from the waters, is all about justice, and this is the climate in which he grows up. His privileges do not render him indifferent to the fate of his people, for it is as both a free man and a comrade that he takes up the defense of one of his Hebrew brothers (Exod 2:11–12).

Intimately associated with the drama-filled destiny of her younger sibling, it was possible for Miriam to discover the presence of God hidden at the heart of history. Courageously and boldly she takes on the role of intermediary. She becomes adept at intervening effectively at the most opportune times. When the Hebrews are enslaved by imperial power, reduced to the state of beasts of burden, Miriam does not at all hesitate to choose a woman from the oppressor's family to collaborate with her in freeing her people.

As in a Mirror, the Other Mary

The destiny to which Miriam is called— a prophetic vocation, a messianic vocation— is, and remains, unique. However, as in a mirror, we already see the calling of another woman being formed. Centuries later a young Jewish girl from an obscure village of Galilee, who is also called Miriam (Mary), will bear a son who will be the Savior of the world.

In her experience we find the same sufferings and flight abroad, to Egypt no less, this time in order to escape the massacre of male infants ordered by King Herod (Matt 2:13–16). In both instances we see a young woman grappling with the forces of death. Both alike have put their trust in the Spirit of life who speaks in them, leads them, each in terms of her own story, on a path that they certainly would not have chosen by themselves.

They are counterparts, two facets of salvation history, these two mothers in Israel, Miriam and Mary.

2. SING GOD'S GLORIOUS TRIUMPH

"He [that is, God] looked upon the Israelites and knew . . ." (Exod 2:25; NAB). The verb "know" in Hebrew expresses a deep union between two beings, their total attachment. God does not simply hear the cries of the Hebrews. God enters into the intimacy of their history. From the midst of the people a liberator will emerge. As Miriam had predicted to her parents, God chooses Moses. It is he who will intervene with Pharaoh to free his people (Exod 3–4).

Pharaoh's Army Drowned

But the ruler who sits at the top of a pyramid of death is not going to let such advantageous manpower leave so easily. He will hang on until the tenth plague, the death of the first-born of the Egyptians, an echo of his own decree of death, before finally permitting the Hebrews to leave the land of slavery (Exod 5–11).

After the institution of the first Passover feast, there begins a long and difficult journey. Chased by Pharaoh and his army, the Hebrews have to flee. A pillar of cloud by day, a pillar of fire by night, the divine presence accompanies them right up to the dramatic moment when the Red Sea closes back upon their pursuers who are directly behind them.

And the midrash says that this is exactly the time the women of the Hebrews get out their tambourines, for they had left Egypt so confident in the future that they had brought along their musical instruments. Saved from the waters, the people burst into their joyful song of victory.

With Tambourines

On the bank of the Red Sea it seems in fact that there are two songs that rise to celebrate "the great work that the Lord did" (Exod 14:31). But while the song of Moses and the sons of Israel extends over nineteen verses (15:1–18), Miriam's and the women's song accounts for only a single verse (Exod. 15:21). Are we to imagine that their enthusiasm would have been so temperate?

This disproportion puts us once again in the presence of one of the "great silences of the Bible," as Judith Plaskow calls them. As women, she says, we have an intuitive awareness of being present at the great foundational moments of history, but it is men who put these events into writing. Since their transcription reflects an essentially masculine personal experience, the women then become invisible. Judith Plaskow deduces from this that Scripture, the written version of the story, is necessarily partial. She expresses this reality by the suggestive and bold image of a "half of Torah," as has already been mentioned. In the Torah nearly the whole lived experience of women, the other half of humanity, is missing.

In the text that conveys the people's victory song to us, we cannot say that women are entirely invisible: they are just relegated to the background. There is that one verse, a single verse!

Mixed Choir

How do we read this silence? Hillel, the great first-century CE Talmudist, suggests to us a first hypothesis. He writes:

> Participate in the community while bearing the yoke imposed by the government with fasting and prayer. The Talmud teaches: If anyone separates from the community, the guardian angels that accompany every person (Ps 91:11–13) lay their hands on his head and say: Whoever is separated from the community cannot participate in the consolation of the community. In contrast, whoever remains associated with the community enjoys consolation, as it is written: "Rejoice with Jerusalem, and be glad for her, all you who love her; rejoice with her in joy, all you who have participated in her struggles" (Isa 66:10).

Thus when Miriam and all her women take up the first stanza of the song of Moses, it shows that they clearly do not want to be separated from the community. They participate fully in the Hebrews' adventure in the wilderness, just as they contributed, at the peril of their lives, to rescuing the male infants in Egypt. With the whole people they bore the yoke of slavery, and with the whole people they now share the difficulties and joys, even though the text leaves them in the shadows of the story.

We could also take the stanza sung by the women as a refrain chanted after each stanza of the men's song. Then we would have two choirs in joyful dialogue about the victory over Pharaoh.

One final supposition—we could imagine that it was the women who first intoned the song, to the sound of the instruments they carried out of Egypt. Carried along by this enthusiasm, the men then joined in this hymn of victory, as it is written: "Then Moses and the Israelites sang this song to the Lord" (Exod 15:1).

The Way out of Silence

These various attempts at an interpretation of one of the great "silences of the Bible" give us the chance to let the personal experience of women in a founding moment in the story finally come to light. It is not so much a question of choosing one reading at the expense of others, but rather of keeping them all together. In the end they are not mutually exclusive; they offer complementary clarifications of an event experienced differently according to whether one is a man or a woman.

On the shore of the Red Sea, the entire people, no one excluded, expresses its thanks for meeting up safe and sound on the other side. All have passed from slavery to freedom, from silence to speech, for according to Rashi, the Hebrew word for Passover, can also be read to mean "the mouth speaks."

If "Passover" evokes a twofold liberation, coming out of oppression and entering the world of speech, then the song of Miriam means a real possibility for the women to come out of silence. It therefore has a prophetic dimension. So it should be noted that this hymn presents Miriam in the role as a prophet, with all the attributes proper to her state: instrumental music, dance, and song (Exod 15:20). This song celebrates the exit from a twofold slavery: the slavery under Pharaoh and the slavery under patriarchy. For women it prefigures the eternal possibility of coming out of all the Egypt's that keep them in silence . . .

A Place to Win

It is astonishing that there is not a trace of Miriam's name in the first two chapters of Exodus. She is always referred to by the word "sister," understood to be the sister of the future hero Moses. A female individual has no proper identity in the patriarchal culture even as a child. Her presence and role are always determined by her relation to her father, or husband, or brother. It is only near the end of the flight from Egypt (Exod 15) that she, whose intervention was so decisive, finds her identity. There she is finally called a "prophet," a qualification weakened however by the words that follows: "The prophet Miriam, Aaron's sister . . ." Even in her role as guide at the head of the daughters of Israel, she is kept in a state of dependence (Exod 15:20). We should note that the biblical text never calls Moses Miriam's brother, even though it is thanks to her that he plays any role in the story at all.

With Miriam nothing seems to be obvious. Even if God chose her from childhood to restart the story, she has to win the place that ought to belong to her by right. No generosity for the women certainly. However, in examining the text closely, we find just enough traces so that we can carve out a biblical space for the feminine.

For example, it is interesting to notice that the Talmud connects wise women with midwives when it defines a person who sees what will be born as wise. (The French language offers a similar connection, as one of its words for midwife carries the literal meaning of "wise woman.") This capacity of anticipating the future is often connected with the kind of knowledge gained by wit and intuition. This is also what characterizes the prophet, and the capable wife described in the book of Proverbs (Prov 31:10–31).

This shouldn't surprise us when we consider the important role wisdom plays in the Scriptures. Both in grammar and in the imagination the Hebrew word for "wisdom" is a feminine expression. Moreover, wisdom is a woman and a prophet (Prov 1:20–33; 8:1–36). It was by her that earth came to be (Prov 8:22–31).

But the Hebrew word does not only mean wisdom, for it is also used in the field of ethics, and there it means good conduct. Likewise in psychology and logic it means "intelligence." It also refers to the special knowledge of artisans, artists, and midwives, of any licensed or inspired individual. Miriam certainly fits into this category, as do the rest of the women of the Hebrews, and many others besides.

Finally, we should also note that in the book of Proverbs one of the personifications of wisdom calls her "sister" (Prov 7:4). So when the prophet Miriam is presented as the sister of Moses and Aaron, there is nothing to prevent our bypassing the simple blood relationship and considering her in her full stature as a woman of God, acknowledging that she has indeed won her place.

3. FAMILY CONFLICTS

Life in the wilderness is a test for the Hebrews on their journey. There they discovered the humanity of each individual, as well as the collective responsibility the group had for all its members. This laborious journey assumes its meaning for Israel at the foot of Sinai where it receives the revelation of the Law: the Decalogue, literally, the "Ten Words," the reminder of God's deliverance, and in consequence an ethical demand which, while it certainly calls for obedience, represents as well a way by which each woman, each man is invited to imitate God.

During this time of restructuring when Moses tries hard to organize the people into a community on the basis of the "Ten Words," Miriam is not mentioned once. Women remain invisible. Even when the purity prescriptions, which touch them most closely, are set forth, it all goes on outside their purview.

By Solidarity or by Deception

It is only in chapter 12 of the book of Numbers that Miriam appears next. It is a very muddled situation where we learn that Miriam and Aaron are criticizing their brother Moses because of the Cushite woman whom he has married. The commentaries are divided on this woman's identity. Some think it is Zipporah, the wife Moses married at the time of the flight into Midian (Exod 2:21)—Cushite normally signifies Nubian or Ethiopian, but sometimes also Midianite (cf. Hab 3:7). Others find her to be a second wife. In this latter case we can understand Miriam's criticism as a gesture of solidarity with the sister–in–law she knew, who had borne the hard crossing of the desert with all the people.

Learning that her brother has just remarried, Miriam cannot stop herself from expressing reprobation.

What then is Miriam's sin that merits the severe punishment of being made a leper? Certainly not her act of solidarity with Zipporah. According to Jewish tradition, her sin was to mix in matters that were not her affair. Moses had to have important reasons to take a second wife, a common custom of the time, and it was no concern of either his brother or his sister to enmesh themselves in his business.

God Works Matters Out

But was that justification for such a punishment? A question all the more important when Miriam and Aaron's intervention ultimately bears on quite another matter. Alongside their brother, they claim fully their role as prophets. Micah confirms this later when he reports the words of the Lord: "I sent before you Moses, Aaron, and Miriam" (Mic 6:4).

It is probably a question of a power struggle born of a feeling of injustice or deception: "Has the Lord spoken only through Moses? Has he not spoken through us also?" Num 12:2). In the face of such a reaction, which not only disturbs family relationships but undermines the authority of the very one who leads the people to the Promised Land, God brings the three of them together as if to hand down a sentence. In wishing to insure her rightful place, Miriam taints not only Moses, but herself as well.

Is the Leprosy a Punishment?

However, even though God's explanation is understandable (Num 12:5–8), the sickness that suddenly strikes Miriam remains troubling, resembling as it does an almost automatic punishment. Besides, one cannot help wondering why it is only Miriam who is afflicted with leprosy. Aaron was in agreement with his sister in speaking against Moses, as he acknowledges only a few verses later: "Do not punish us for a sin we have so foolishly committed" (v. 11).

Numerous commentators justly point out that the text says that Miriam was the first to criticize Moses' second marriage, but we have just suggested that her reaction could be justified by her affection for her sister-in-law Zipporah. Whatever it is, Miriam is afflicted with a sickness, which in that era resulted in exclusion for its victims. "[P]ut out of the camp everyone who is leprous . . . both male and female" (Num 5:2–3; cf. Lev 13:45–46).

As White as Snow

In Miriam's case it is said not only that she had leprosy, but that she was "as white as snow" (Num 12:10). This expression often evokes the idea of purity (as in Ps 51:9) and seems counter to the notion of leprosy. It does reflect, however, the strange declaration in Leviticus: "But if the disease breaks out in the skin, so that it covers all the skin of the diseased person from head to foot, so far as the priest can see, then the priest shall make an examination, and if the disease has covered all his body, he shall pronounce him clean of the disease; since it has all turned white, he is clean" (Lev 13:12–13).

To understand this text, we return to the time when the departure from Egypt was imminent. God had revealed his Name and his divine power to Moses (Exod 3–4). He had given him three signs of it: the staff, leprosy, and water (Exod 4:2–9). Concerning leprosy, we know that Moses' hand had become "leprous, the color of snow," but that it had returned to normal right away. By this sign God gave him a stronger and more enduring message than a simple word.

So Miriam's leprosy, "as white as snow," reminds us of her brother's. It is more a sign than a disease. This is why Miriam alone is afflicted with it. The two other signs, the staff and water, will also result in exclusion when their turn comes. Aaron and Moses will be their victims, and they will not be able to enter the Promised Land (Num 20:1–13).

Seven Days of Exclusion

While the leprosy that struck Miriam is in the first place a sign, like all leprosy it involves being quarantined. However, this quarantine will not exceed seven days. The reason for the exception is given to Moses. Miriam receives only a father's disapproval, again signified by an image that in our day we find shocking: "If her father had but spit in her face, would she not bear her shame for seven days?" (Num 12:14). This is a gesture used to humiliate someone publicly (cf. Deut 25:9) and is all the more expressive when one is in an oral culture.

Seven days of exclusion, seven days that God gives Miriam for meditating, listening, understanding. Seven days, the period of time from one Sabbath to another, recalling the seven days of creation. In order for this sign to play its freeing and recreating role, it has to be correctly interpreted. These seven days seem to be a necessary minimum of solitude for Miriam to start over again under the divine tutelage.

Everyone Waited for Her

Is it not amazing to read that, right at that time, the Hebrews find themselves halted in the hostile wilderness? Everything happens as though there were a common destiny for the prophet Miriam and the people. Perhaps the people are expecting something important to happen in the life of this woman even though she does not appear to represent a very great force in a patriarchal society. The people's being immobilized at this moment seems to point to the strong solidarity which unites them with Miriam, momentarily cast onto the margin of the story. Then we learn that Miriam's death at Kadesh will be accompanied by a total lack of water there (Num 20:1–2). The midrash makes specific mention that it is thanks to Miriam's merits that a well assuaged the Hebrews' thirst, a well which did not dry up while she was in their midst.

Perhaps it is interesting to recall in this connection that the well associated with her, while a well is always a source of life and joy in the Bible, is also a source of understanding—the Hebrew word which means "well" as the same root as a verb which means "to explain." So we can imagine this forced halt in the wilderness as a time of growth and re-examination of what happened at Mount Sinai. It can even be said that it was necessary in order that the freely accepted covenant relationship find a way to be realized in the daily life of both individuals and the community.

Once Miriam has again taken her place in the midst of the Hebrews, they consent to resume their journey. And we hear nothing more of her. Silence again envelopes her. It is only when they arrive at the wilderness of Zin that she reappears, but she is then near death.

4. HER DEATH IN THE WILDERNESS

All the major events in Miriam's life are associated with water. On the banks of the Nile she saves Moses. On the shore of the Red Sea she celebrates the rescue of the Hebrews with a song. According to midrashic tradition it is thanks to her merits that a well accompanies the people in their journey across the desert. And at the time of her death it is again a matter of water, but this time it is lacking.

There Is no More Water to Drink

It is the first of the month of Nisan, the month when they celebrate Passover (Exod 12:1). The Hebrews have reached the wilderness of Zin, and they settle down at Kadesh. Miriam has arrived at the end of her long journey (Num 20:1). Could there be a better place to meet God? The place name Kadesh means "to sanctify" in Hebrew, and sanctification is the act of connecting the earthly and the heavenly, the human and the divine.

In this month of Passover, which represents the ultimate passage for Miriam, she disappears from the story once and for all, and with her the water disappears too. In death she carries off the sign that had accompanied her during her entire life as a prophet. She disappears totally but gives way to a new experience of the power of God. Water will not be lacking, but it will take on a new meaning. It will no longer be bound up with Miriam's presence, but instead with Moses' staff.

Lacking water, the people murmur against Moses yet again. He takes Aaron with him to seek counsel in the tent of meeting (20:6). God commands him to take his staff and with his brother assemble the community in front of "the rock before their eyes" (20:8) and command it to yield water. Just speaking to the rock will be enough to bring the water out of it.

Moses' Anger

Moses does not obey God's command scrupulously however. Instead of speaking to the rock, he speaks to the people: "Listen, you rebels, shall we bring water for you out of this rock?" (Num 20:10). Giving way to anger, he then strikes the rock. The Bible is not afraid of showing the shadow side of the great heroes of the faith. We had noted this with Miriam. The same is true in the case of Moses.

This kind of reaction on Moses' part can be explained as one component in the difficulty of heading up a people who often pick quarrels with him. Furthermore, speaking to a rock in front of them is not the action of a serious person. Striking it is certainly a more manly gesture. It would not be hard to find excuses for Moses, but Torah does not give him even one. For having disbelieved God, he is excluded from the number of those who will enter the land of promise (20:12), as Miriam formerly had been momentarily excluded from the community.

In addition, we can see in Moses' behavior the consequences of the shock caused by Miriam's death. In fact how can he not be struck by the coincidence of her death and the lack of water? The people's murmuring recalls the primordial place that Miriam occupied in the community. Moses must have felt suddenly very much alone, to the point of being unmindful of God. "Shall we bring you something to drink?" he asks, whereas they would rather wait to hear him resume speaking to God as he used to do (Exod 16:8). All this seems to be proof that his sister's death had affected him profoundly.

Like a Gushing Spring

If Miriam had not intervened on the banks of the Nile, Moses would have died young. Having been saved from the water, he was to become aware that water has a twofold meaning. It guarantees survival but can also cause death. He had had that experience twice: first, when he was a baby, second, in a much more conscious way of course, while passing through the Red Sea.

In the symbolic order, water is connected more with the feminine than the masculine by the natural connection of water and life and woman. Perhaps this explains why Moses has not completely understood the meaning of this sign.

Perhaps we can say that this lack of understanding points to the absence of any recognition of the role played by women, of whom Miriam was the privileged representative. Everything happens as if women did not exist. This is an exclusion that impoverishes the community and even puts it in peril.

With Miriam's death the visible sign that showed her place in the community visibly and concretely disappears. And it is perhaps only at that moment that Moses becomes conscious of what his sister's life meant for him and for the whole people. If water was flowing in abundance and slaking their thirst, it was because Miriam had known how to redeem the time during her seven days retreat. She had turned their forced halt to good account in order to restore, renew, recreate her relationship with God. This was why the water had not failed.

But who then had been able to comprehend that it was through the mediation of his prophet Miriam that God was present in the midst of his people like a gushing spring?

2

Hannah the Visionary

WHILE THE STORY OF Samuel is relatively familiar to us, his mother's is probably much less so. However, this woman played an important role, in fact an essential role at a decisive moment in her people's history.

Indeed the great turning points of the biblical narrative almost always have at their origin a person who not only considers events with both amazement and forbearance, but still looks for a way to emerge from the situation. Hannah—woman, spouse, prophet, and mother—belongs to this category of women and men of faith without whom God seemingly could not put history back into the dynamism of the Torah.

1. REBELLING AGAINST FATE

After the long and hard journey through the wilderness, the Hebrews settled in the country God had promised them in exchange for their faithfulness to the covenant (Exod 34:10–13). The people very quickly forget their commitment however and let themselves be seduced by the worship of Baal and Astarte (Judg 2:1–3). Instead of jealously preserving their identity, they choose idolatry and assimilation.

When Hannah enters the story, the period of the judges is ending. Settlement in Canaan has presented Israel with a hard test from which it does not emerge completely unscathed. Thanks to strong personalities like Deborah, Gideon, and Samson, the twelve tribes tried to preserve their unity as best they could. After the horrible surrender of the Benjamites at Gibeah (Judg 19), the situation deteriorated to the point where the book of Judges ends with this wry remark: "In those days there was no king in Israel; all the people did what was right in their own eyes" (Judg 21:25).

She Who Was Barren

From the beginning of 1 Samuel, we learn that Hannah was a member of that group of women whom patriarchal society marginalized. In fact her sterility reduces her to the role of an unproductive and therefore useless person (1 Sam 1:2). As was done at the time of her sisters the matriarchs, her husband Elkanah has taken a second wife, Peninnah.

At this time a couple's sterility—really the sterility of the woman, for no man is ever depicted as barren in the Bible!—constitutes a tough ordeal. Finding it impossible to fulfill their procreative vocation puts them in a discriminatory position, whence Elkanah's choice—in the end he had no other—to take that second wife.

The commandment to "be fruitful and multiply" (Gen 1:28) has been understood almost exclusively across the centuries as the duty of bringing children into the world. Yet Jewish tradition reads it with a spiritual meaning too: by respecting that which is of God in others, the whole earth could be filled with God's presence. So there is more than one way to "be fruitful and multiply." But at this time it was the literal reading that prevailed, and so Hannah could only have a negative self-image.

As in the adventure of Abraham's wife Sarah in the harem of Abimelech, God has often been considered as the giver and taker of fertility (Gen 20:17), "the guardian of the uterus" in Jewish tradition. A barren wife's sadness and suffering are even harder to deal with when her state seems to be the expression of God's will or even a punishment from heaven (Gen 30:2).

In Hannah's case it turns out a bit differently. Certainly her suffering cannot be denied. No woman under those conditions can live lightly with sterility. But for all that, must she let herself be marginalized? Is there not another way that makes sense of her life? These are questions Hannah had to ask herself not only as a wife, but also as a prophet—as we have seen, she is a member of the group of the seven women in whom the Talmud recognizes the gift of prophecy.

Another Suffering

Her suffering therefore is not caused solely by sterility, but stems also, perhaps even more, from the interpretation given to it, from the overstatement of which she is the object.

Elkanah has not divorced Hannah. Although childless, she continues as a beloved and cherished wife, so much so that Elkanah's attentions toward her arouse the jealousy of her rival (1 Sam 1:5–7). She and her husband are a united couple and share a united spiritual life. Together each year they go up to the sanctuary at Shiloh.

In spite of the developing assimilation all around them, they remain faithful to their ancestral ways. Their faithfulness is so alive that God receives a particular name for the first time: "the Lord of hosts" (1 Sam 1:3), which evokes the God of the armies ("hosts") of heaven and earth, the God who brought the people out of Egypt, the God of whom Deborah sang so magnificently (Judg 5:1–31).

In those days however the sons of Eli the priest are treating God contemptuously. They do not hesitate to keep aside for their own use the better parts of the sacrifices the pilgrims offer (1 Sam 2:12–17, 29), and Hannah does not remain insensitive to this matter. She weeps because she understands that her barrenness is a reflection of the barrenness of her people. There is a symbolic connection between her personal humiliation and the degraded cult at Shiloh. All her husband Elkanah's love cannot prevent the tears from flowing, but he does not understand what they mean.

The sadness of prophets is often lonely. Only those who share such sadness understand it. This is why Hannah leaves her town to go up to the sanctuary, where she knows she will receive a welcome and understanding.

Victimized by and Complicit in the System, Both

The way Hannah manages to live with her sterility illuminates the strategic possibilities open to women as they forge a way through patriarchal structures. However, it involves making a choice. So the narrative confronts us with two options: either to submit like Peninnah or to rebel like Hannah.

Two women, two choices. On the one hand, Peninnah: surrounded by a nursery of children she fits nicely as the image of the ideal woman in a patriarchal society. Although a second wife, the house of Elkanah depends on her. Busy raising her daughters and sons, she does not ask herself all that many questions. At the very most she is somewhat jealous of her rival, which is understandable, given Elkanah's affection for Hannah.

What shocks us in Peninnah's attitude is her way of provoking Hannah, mocking her suffering (1 Sam 1:6). Of course she is not the first in history to behave that way. We remember the young Hagar deriding Sarah, still barren in old age (Gen 16:4–5).

Peninnah certainly is not conscious of the social meaning of her scoffing. She does not understand that, although integrated into society, she is nonetheless also its victim. Such is the perversity of the system that even women who fulfill their role perfectly are not accepted and respected as equals of the men.

Thus Peninnah does not realize that the place she occupies is in reality only a splendid prison. She is only there thanks to her numerous pregnancies. Society sees her as a fertile womb and not an autonomous person with a proper identity and the freedom of action. In this role Peninnah is an unconscious victim.

As soon as she begins to deride Hannah's suffering and humiliation, however, she is no longer society's victim and becomes its accomplice. By failing in solidarity, by making separate cause in order to hang onto power, by adopting the male norms, she is actively upholding the established order. When she dares to speak, it is not so that she might express her own ideas, but instead in order to repeat the ideas that go down well in a society based on inequality of the sexes. She is both victim and complicit in her own victimization, not knowing how to accept the invitation made to her: "Arise, my love . . . and come away" (Song 2:10). Come away and seize the freedom to become who you are, a free woman.

She Rises

Hannah, however, does rise up (1 Sam 1:9). The very vigor of her act emphasizes her determination to renounce her tears and to envision a future. In order to do that, she awakens the sparks of life that sadness had swept under the ashes. The meaning of her name comes back to mind: Hannah means "favor," or "grace," which in Hebrew literally means the act of leaning toward someone to show that person your interest or affection. What could this woman, shut up in a metaphor that she had not chosen, take from her name?

Having a name means not only being able to let oneself be called, but likewise being able to answer, "Here I am," in a tradition that goes back to Abraham and that is likewise characteristic of servants. So Hannah rises and decides to enter upon a call and response dialogue in an effort to inscribe the way of life contained in her name into history.

In the climate of corruption that was tarnishing the Shiloh sanctuary at the time (1 Sam 2:12–17), a woman arose to live out her identity. If Hannah had not been able to bear a child up to that day, in the future she will be a bearer of grace.

This is a prophetic act. Her rebellion allows her to break out of the prison of the barren woman and reconsider her situation. Sterility is not only the lot of women put at a disadvantage by nature. In Hannah's case she finds herself in community with the children of Israel who have turned aside from the covenant of Sinai, as well as with the priests of Shiloh who practice their debaucheries at the very entrance of the tent of meeting (1 Sam 2:22).

Hannah seems to know intuitively that she must write a page of grace into history. This page of grace will not be simply a stereotypically feminine, sweet, and modest welcome, but rather a welcome of firmness, determination, and creativity, as well as of denunciation, interrogation, and rebellion. She will do it her way, not with warlike violence, but with a song that will become a model for the annunciation of every shaking of the foundations (1 Sam 2:1–10; cf. Luke 1:46–55). But before going into action, she must find, or perhaps recover, her identity, her face: not her physical face, but courageous resistance in order to face and confront the judgment of the patriarchy.

Giving, Over and Over Again

So Hannah withdraws into the sanctuary at Shiloh. This is no imposing temple. At that time God lived in the midst of the people in a fragile habitation, in a sort of tent. In the shape of the nomad dwelling, the space the Ark occupied offered a spot where one could find rest, could regain one's strength, or just enjoy being with God. Anyone was free to go there unannounced to honor the covenant of Sinai.

Upon going in, Hannah is certain she will find a Presence to speak with, a Presence that will answer her. She prays to God calling out that new name, "Lord of hosts" (1 Sam 1:11).

In the privacy of the tent of meeting, Hannah experiences faith as a form of companionship, a long voyage with the One who is at once judge, counsel for the defense, and lover. This is an adventure that does not come without shared risk and free consent by both parties. But it is also an adventure in which God raises Hannah to the rank of dialogue partner.

Like Abraham before her (Gen 18:27–33), Hannah does not hesitate to strike a deal with God: "If you will only look on the misery of your servant" (1 Sam 1:11), yes, if you are really, as you say, tender and merciful, "give to your servant a male child." Make it so that my family and social situation change in my favor. In return, I will give this boy back to you. He will be at your service until the day he dies.

Much More than the Desire for a Child

Is it not surprising to see a mother dispose of the life of a son yet to be born in this way? It certainly is not the first time that a woman is constrained to do such bargaining. But are we here solely in the presence of a mother who pledges the future of her child in order to gain standing in society?

Words and actions usually have several meanings in the prophets. Therefore, for Hannah the desire for a child does not exhaust the meaning of her vow. If she is looking for a way to change her situation, it is not simply a question of gaining the status of mother. By her vow—which, moreover, she pronounces without the consent of her husband (cf. Num 30:14–16)—she wants to prove that the laws and customs by which women are excluded are not necessarily true reflections of the divine will. So she challenges both God and the patriarchy!

There is no question but that the birth of Samuel will agree with her. "Elkanah knew his wife Hannah, and the Lord remembered her" (1 Sam 1:19). Fortunately for us women, the biblical narrative does not always affirm the dominant way of thinking!

The story of Hannah shows too that sterility can become a prophetic sign. The inability to give life can be reflective of the sterility of society. As later in the time of Hosea who will be ordered to marry a prostitute (Hos 1:2), in order to open closed minds, a sign that speaks loud and strong is needed—that of "the barren [who] has borne seven" (1 Sam 2:5).

2. SPIRITUAL JOURNEY

It is with a wounded body that Hannah enters the sanctuary, conscious that her suffering is not only caused by the absence of a child and Peninnah's contempt, but just as much by the social and religious situation of her people. She came there to look for the freedom to love her wounded body and recall her identity, along with the covenant and promise which are part of that identity.

This step in the restoration of the depth of her being will be done in accord with the very layout of the sanctuary. Even though the architecture is still very simple at Shiloh, its interior arrangement is already an education in itself.

The space includes the holy place, and the altar within, then the table with the bread of the Presence on the north side, and across from it on the south side the seven-branched lampstand. Finally, separated by a veil, the most holy place with the ark of the covenant (cf. Exod 25–27).

The text that recounts Hannah's approach is very succinct. It only tells us that she "wept bitterly" and made a prayer and vow to God (1 Sam 1:10–11). However, Eli's words suggest that Hannah has taken her time with her orisons and that such behavior had probably become unusual at Shiloh.

Her Prayer to Find Herself

Whereas at the time of Jesus women could only enter the court of the Temple which was reserved for them, in Hannah's time they could still participate in worship directly, and it doesn't seem that any parts of the sanctuary were forbidden them. Hannah therefore does not need the intermediary of a priest to pray to God. Inside the sanctuary she feels free to act according to her needs and her intuition.

Eli remained outside. Since the text presents us with an open space, we will try to fill it by imagining what Hannah has been through in the course of this experience.

First, she prays across from the altar. She raises her heart with her hands uplifted (Lam 3:41). Her hands with their ten fingers are an image of the two tables of the law and the Decalogue itself, and they remind her of her own moral task, at the same time confronting her with the near impossibility of accomplishing it. Before the altar of sacrifice she takes time to listen to what her body, her wounded being, tells her. From this prayerful listening slowly rises the awareness that her freedom has been alienated, and that the condemnation of society that weighs her down obscures her mind and her heart.

In the silence of the sanctuary Hannah sadly realizes that it is not she, but rather the barren woman, who is praying. That label sticks as it were to her skin and imposes a role on her that in no way corresponds to who she is in her deepest being. This is a revolutionary discovery, and it confirms the rightness of the step she has taken.

But however freeing it is, rebellion alone does not suffice. The process of liberation must continue on in the abandonment of this role to the One who has heard her prayer. By a symbolic gesture, by means of the prayer of a heart that is both poor and proud, Hannah leaves her mask as a woman without a child on the altar so as finally to enter into a deeper relationship with herself. It is thanks to this letting-go that she can leave to explore her true identity.

It is as though Hannah must "repent and turn away from" (Ezek 14:6) what has become a societal idol, namely, that a woman fulfills the purpose of her creation only by bearing children. The Hebrew notion of repentance here is not to accuse oneself or others, but rather to make an about-face in the midst of a community gone wrong and return to the original intention of God who "created humankind in his image" (Gen 1:27).

Together with God she goes off to explore who she really is, "created in [God's] image." This means, as was stated earlier, in the section "She Rises," that she will recover her identity insofar as she learns the form of resistance with which she will henceforth contrast the image that others make of her with her true identity, revealed in this prayer experience.

In Solidarity with her People

At the heart of her prayer, Hannah has had the opportunity to realize how much her mind was blocked, her freedom alienated, and her will destroyed by a society that granted no place to a woman without a child.

In her case, as we have said, sterility does not just provoke a personal sadness. To her already obscured, hidden, and distorted identity there is added a perhaps more intimate and certainly more secret wound. Does she not see in her wounded body the reflection of the ill-being that afflicts the Israelites with sterility as well?

This is the suffering of the prophet who sees her people leave off following the Torah. Hannah feels the faithlessness in her body. As a prophet she cannot escape the nagging question: how can she teach the women and men of her day how to live in the Promised Land and be faithful to the God of Sinai? She certainly sees the same events that her contemporaries do, but with this difference, that she sees into them so deeply that she can identify them with her own affliction.

In the search for her inmost being the pedagogy of the tent of meeting leads Hannah to where the table with the bread of the Presence and the lampstand with seven branches are. These are two cult objects to be sure, but they are also two objects that symbolize the human being in both the spiritual and social dimension. As she approaches them, Hannah chooses to be a woman who can stand her ground. She is ready to take the necessary steps to bring her inmost identity to realization and to reconstruct her being as a woman. Does this attitude not anticipate that of the thousands of pilgrims who, across the centuries and in all religions, walk a labyrinth, borne along by the hope of reaching that place of rest and inspiration where the divine and the human meet heart to heart?

Face to Face

On the table of acacia wood with gold molding are two rows of six loaves with pure frankincense placed with each row (Lev 24:5–7). In biblical language incense often symbolizes the movement that rises to God from the depth of one's being. Joy is also a part of this dynamic interpretation, the joy of a heart that knows in advance that it is accepted and welcomed (Ezek 20:40–41).

Sweet-smelling perfume with soothing scent, the incense set with the two rows of loaves invites her to the encounter. God responds to Hannah's search "face to face" so that she can, in her turn, encounter others face to face. This is what the loaves suggest, for they are literally "the bread of the Presence" (Exod 25:30). The smoke of the incense, from which rises the scent of hope, is the slender and ethereal sign that leaves Hannah soothed by the certainty that her connection with God is restored at the same time that her inner being is rebuilt.

Here she is, ready to take on her prophetic name, ready to be a sign of "grace" in the midst of her contemporaries. Therefore, after having rediscovered the breath of life alongside the table with the loaves, she can be on her way and move to the seven-branched lampstand made of pure gold.

Being a Light

If the lampstand represents the human being standing up, tradition first sees in it an image of Torah or, better yet, the light of Torah. It symbolizes the human being as bearer of the particular light that flows from these seven cups filled with oil. As the number "seven" indicates, it is a matter of a messianic light. Every human being bears a spark of this light within, and it is this light that molds the human being into the image of God. However, each person remains free to use that light in the service of others or to hide it, even free to extinguish it.

Alongside the lampstand Hannah can see that the light coming forth from the pure olive oil gives "light on the space in front of it" (Exod 25:37). So a future is possible after all, a pathway for other forms of sociability, other forms of relationship. In this new light Hannah feels free to occupy her own social space. She remakes herself as a "being-with" (i.e., "being-with-others," in the Heideggerian sense), a person humanly engaged with another. As it is written, "It is not good that [a person] should be alone" (Gen 2:18).

Passing from the table with the bread of the Presence to the light of the lampstand, Hannah discovers the light of the divine face as a kindly force, which is given to her in order that she may be light, in order that she may write her own identity into human history. Where could she better restore meaning to her life than in the sanctuary near the ark of the covenant?

Hannah the barren one, Hannah the rejected, but also Hannah the bearer of grace, Hannah the prophet—from now on she is entirely free to engage in a partnership with

God. She is no longer alone; her strength and her desires are bound up with God's strength and desires.

Perhaps for the first time in her life she feels her body as a wonder that permits her to be entirely herself. Her joy is so great her praise so expressive that old Eli seated at the gate of the sanctuary, does not recognize her and takes her for a drunken stranger. Such a mistake says a lot about the spirit then reigning at Shiloh!

3. THE SON GIVEN

On her return to the village, "Elkanah knew his wife Hannah, and the Lord remembered her" (1 Sam 1:19). As the days passed, Hannah the barren one becomes Hannah the mother. Hannah gives birth to a son whom she calls Samuel so that no one forgets that this child is a gift of God, a prayer made flesh—it means what she says, "I have asked him of the Lord" according to popular etymology (1:20).

Therefore Samuel is not like any other child. Not only has God taken a decisive part in his birth; even more, well before he is born, his mother made him a nazarite, like Samson (Judg 13:5; 16:17), a man entirely consecrated to God and living with a particular mission. From before his birth Samuel is vowed to the service of God.

The Time to Become a Sign of Grace

Samuel is not an ordinary child, and his mother is no ordinary mother! With what could have seemed a shocking decision, she chooses a special education for her son. According to her vow he is to be raised according to nazarite rules: the razor will not touch his head, and he will taste neither wine nor strong drink (Num 6:3–5), a way of life opposite to that of the sons of Eli, who behave like scoundrels (1 Sam 2:12–17).

In vowing him to the service of God for the rest of his life, Hannah takes real liberty in deciding his future. In our age, when a child's freedom has been erected into law, such an attitude might appear shocking. But in Hannah's situation one understands it. And one notices as well that she freely takes on its consequences: early separation from this son she has so much desired.

But for the moment Hannah is still caught up in the joy of motherhood. So that Samuel might know a stable and calm life from his first years, she keeps him apart from the perverse atmosphere of Shiloh. So Elkanah goes without her to the sanctuary for the annual sacrifice prescribed by the Law. Hannah will wait until her child is weaned before taking him up to Shiloh and giving him to God (1:22).

Possessive love, a mother's wisdom, or is it the discernment of a prophet? All three certainly. Besides, Hannah needed all that time so that she might perform her act freely, and not solely as the performance of a vow.

This is a time of seclusion, a nazarite time for Hannah herself, who little by little leaves her status as a mother on the personal level for that as a mother on the social and political plane. Following a trail blazed by Miriam and Deborah, Hannah takes her place in this line of women who by their courage and their determination knew how to play the role of "a mother in Israel."

When Hannah prays, it is not to demand a personal favor from her personal God. Instead it is, invoking God by his universal name, "Lord of hosts," in order to become a sign of grace in favor with all her contemporaries (1:11).

When Hannah wishes for a son, she wishes for more than a son. She wishes for a child who will be the sign of God in the midst of the exploding corruption of her time.

Three Women of Hope

With Hannah boundaries become places of creativity and spaces of newness because God is acting in entire freedom. "She gives birth because she is barren," we say paradoxically.

His Mother Made Him a Little Robe

In spite of a happy ending—Hannah will have three more sons and two daughters—her life will remain marked by tragedy. Perhaps more than others, prophets are called to identify acts that can clear away the violence present in every society.

Hannah is one of the righteous ones whose innocence and suffering, expressed symbolically, restore meaning to life. With her this takes the form of a little robe. Every year she sewed a fresh one and took it when she made her pilgrimage to Shiloh. She would put it on Samuel in a way that was full of motherly affection and divine protection (1 Sam 2:18–19).

Reading the signs of her time from the inside, she knows that her son will not have an easy task. In order to confront King Saul, he will have special need to feel the hand of God on his shoulder. The robe will remind him of it. Like Aaron before him who had needed a rod, Hannah understands that Samuel needs a robe, which will become his distinctive sign.

We recall the visit that Saul made to the woman who was a medium in Endor. When she recounts to him her vision of an old man wrapped in a robe, Saul immediately recognizes Samuel, because of this detail. Although he is already dead at the time of this meeting, his robe remained very much alive in his contemporaries' minds (1 Sam 28:14; cf. v. 3).

It is a robe of tenderness, the robe of a prophet. In making it, Hannah foretells Samuel's future without knowing how it will come about. In this special sign, poetry and prophecy are joined with romanticism. By means of this little robe Hannah knew how to raise her attention as a mother to the level of that of the prophet. Between her questioning of her son's future and the actual situation of her time, she wove a connection, which gave birth in time to the robe-symbol of Samuel.

I Will Rejoice in Your Victory

In a poem of praise and victory Hannah celebrates the fulfillment of her vow (1 Sam 2:1–10). Bowed down before God with the little Samuel at her side, she unleashes her free-flowing thanksgiving. She not only is a mother but knows the fullness of motherhood as well: "the barren has borne seven" (v. 5). She can play her creative role, and she can be a bearer of newness in all sectors of life, not simply in the restricted framework reserved by the society of her time for childbearing.

Like Deborah before her, a mother is once more raised up because Israel lacked leaders (cf. Judg 5:7). We find in the song of Hannah the same dynamism that had made her a woman standing on her own two feet and capable of an existential reversal. We find traces in this magnificent poem of her experience in the sanctuary, a unique experience that permits a rebirth from on high.

Hannah's childbearing certainly represents a victory over a personal impossibility. But when God transforms a single human story, does it not affect the whole world as well? Hannah understands it this way. And this is why she turns to him, now in the third person, now the second person. Her poem reflects an intimate experience with God while at the same time preserving a universal range. Her words do not shut God up in the box of a single personal history. This is why, centuries later, Mary would not hesitate to take these words for her song about an equally personal event, the disturbing presence of God in history (Luke 1:46–55). The lowly are lifted up while the bows of the mighty are broken; the barren woman gives birth and the prolific mother withers. The song truly celebrates God as master of a topsy-turvy world.

A Free Woman

Hannah was probably not a witness to the moment when Samuel poured the vial of oil and "the Lord anointed [David] ruler," for that happened many years later (1 Sam 10:1). The fact remains that with Samuel's birth she turns a page of history. As the period of the Judges comes to an end, her son inaugurates the period of the prophets. As the period of the Judges comes to an end, social and political life will be organized in monarchical fashion under the reign of Saul.

In the midst of all these upheavals Hannah put her entire person at the service of God and her people in order to avoid the divisions that were menacing the Hebrews since the time of their settlement in the land of Canaan and in order to restore monotheistic religion. With her special gifts, and as a woman, she kept a lamp burning at this chaotic time in history.

Her song takes its place in a literary genre that seems particularly suited to women of the Bible. Like Miriam's and Deborah's, this poem, carried along by the breath of the Spirit, recalls that there is no king but God, that the only link capable of safeguarding the unity of the people is faithfulness to God.

In ending, let us emphasize that this song recalls to us the truth that we do have limits. In that it is typically feminine. When Hannah proclaims that "the barren has borne seven," she can do it because judgment belongs to God, not to humans.

Wife, mother, prophet, completely respecting the law of her time, Hannah gives us the exemplar of a free woman. Free to inscribe her identity as a woman onto history and onto life.

3

Huldah the Townswoman

Around four centuries have passed. A new prophet will now play a determining role in Israel's history. Her name is Huldah (2 Kgs 22:14–20). Kings have succeeded the judges; empires rise and fall according to the rhythm of the over-weening ambition of their rulers. In the kingdom of Judah we find a spiritually and morally corrupt environment, which had already affected Hannah's life so profoundly.

In a Climate of Religious Confusion

We are in the second half of the seventh century; Josiah is king (640–49). His reign coincides with the fall of the Assyrian empire and the rise in strength of the Babylonian empire. Josiah will take advantage of this somewhat less menacing situation to resume his great-grandfather Hezekiah's (716–687) policy of religious reform.

When Josiah ascended the throne, he was only eight years old (2 Kgs 22:1). For more than a half a century the prophetic voice had been nearly silent. Under both

Manasseh (687–42) and his son Amon (642–40) the cult of Baal was reintroduced. Both, entirely submissive to Assyrian power, had permitted the worship of all the host of heaven, along with sacred prostitution, both male and female, to be installed in Jerusalem. It is told that Manasseh shed very much innocent blood (2 Kgs 21:16), and there is a tradition that he would have had the prophet Isaiah assassinated.

Either through the massive deportation which the Assyrians effected or because of Manasseh's religious syncretism, the dwindling of any sense of their traditional identity among the people increased year by year. In the midst of these forms of assimilation only a small minority still lived according to Torah and kept intact the old practices of worship and ethical standards. These were principally those whom Zephaniah calls the *anawim*, the poor, the humble, the little ones (Zeph 2:3). As opposed to the universalism founded on violence and Assyria's geographic expansion, these *anawim* posit a universalism founded on Torah: they obey God, they do not threaten the lives of others, they accept the consequences of their faithfulness and respect differences and dialogue. At the same time they consider the Lord of Israel to be the universal God, the only God, not only of his own people but also for all of humankind.

In this confused moral and religious climate Josiah tries to restart the religious reform begun by his great-grandfather Hezekiah. He fights syncretism, especially the attraction of Canaanite culture and cults. In order to emphasize the return to fundamental values, he undertakes the purification and renovation of the Jerusalem temple. In this immense task he is helped by the levitical priests and the prophets. But the determining factor during the work of restoration will prove to be the discovery of a scroll of the Law in 622 (2 Kgs 22:8).

This discovery provides the prophet Huldah with the chance to intervene in a decisive manner in the course of history. By confirming the threats written in the scroll, she authenticates the scroll that the high priest found and, in effect, makes it the primary scriptural authority. So it is a woman who decides the biblical canon!

Famous and Learned

Little information has come down to us about Huldah the person. With the exception of her prophecy, tradition has no other oracles to pass on from her lips. If the books which appeared with their names attached let us form fairly clear ideas of her male colleagues Zephaniah, Jeremiah, and Habakkuk, for Huldah we must content ourselves with a few verses in the middle of the great royal chronicle (2 Kgs 22:14–20; cf. 2 Chr 34:22–28). Then, as we have already done with Miriam and Hannah, we will listen to the silence that surrounds her . . .

The biblical authors are unfortunately usually only too happy to report on women without troubling to quote their words. For example, we do not know what that other Hannah, Simeon's colleague Anna, might have said in her prophecy (Luke 2:36–38). In the case of Huldah on the other hand, it seems that we possess all of her words, which stands as a kind of proof that this woman was out of the ordinary.

It is interesting to note that Huldah is presented to us first as a prophet, and only afterward as the wife of Shallum, a Temple functionary (2 Kgs 22:14). She was almost certainly a member of the affluent class of the population, for she lived in the new quarter, probably in the houses rebuilt for the priests and important functionaries on the heights of Jerusalem. With a little imagination, even whimsical imagination, we can say that she was a friend of the mother of King Josiah. In fact the old queen must have also been a pretty remarkable woman for her son to have had the idea of taking up his great-grandfather's reform. He could not have found such an inspiration in the house of his father Amon or that of his grandfather Manasseh.

So Huldah is a privileged woman, but that does not prevent her from belonging to the group of the *anawim*, that little remnant of faithful believers for whom Torah gives meaning to life. She loves the Word of God, and beyond that she knows it so well that she does not hesitate to identify the book found in the Temple as that very Word. She is also a cultivated woman, well versed in Scripture.

The Longest Prophecy by a Woman

At that time—or just a bit later—Jeremiah was also prophesying. He was renowned for his critical mind. Perhaps the high priest Hilkiah, who had discovered the book, and his secretary Shaphan dreaded what might be the reaction of this "prophet of doom," and so they preferred consulting Huldah. Doubtless they hoped that a woman, especially a woman of the better class, will be less severe.

But Huldah is a prophet first, and her judgment is harsh enough that it could have been Jeremiah's. She does not hesitate to confirm the terrible prediction contained in the book, even if she knows that it will not happen immediately.

Huldah's response comes well within the scope of the prophetical tradition. She expresses herself using the sanctioned phrase of the tradition: "Thus says the Lord" (2 Kgs 22:16,19). The content respects the usual outline: after the denunciations (vv. 16–17) come the consolations (vv. 18–20).

So it is not just a woman's word, but one like that of any prophet, a word of the Lord. And that word is no less severe than one of Jeremiah's would have been. However, she is not as excessive as he could be. With striking, but not shocking, expressions Huldah says clearly what she has to say. Alongside the more exuberant style of a Jeremiah, she brings finesse and discretion to a message that is nonetheless dramatic.

A Warning, Perhaps

It is interesting to note that Huldah's prediction seems to contain a little mistake. She announces to King Josiah (2 Kgs 22:20) that he will be "gathered to his grave in peace." But we know that Josiah will die a violent death at the battle of Megiddo (23:29).

However, is it really a mistake? If it were, the compilers of the Bible could have taken it out. By keeping it, they emphasize the importance they place on the person of Huldah. Her prestige has remained so high that two gates of the Temple are called "Huldah's gates" according to midrashic tradition. No other prophet has such an honor.

We can also make another reading of this "mistake." As a prophet Huldah recognizes and expresses the will of God in a particular situation. She reads through events, but also through human nature. She knows, or at least senses, what can or will happen. On that score we can interpret the prophecy: "You will rest in peace," as a warning to Josiah.

In the way of the prophets, she announces to the king that God will uphold his reform, but that this will entail his living according to the Law. Toward the end of his life, Josiah no longer resisted violence: he refused diplomatic negotiations proposed by the Pharaoh Neco II (2 Chr 35:20–22).

Not following the way God had opened for him, he engaged in a useless war at Megiddo that ended tragically for him.

This military defeat where he met his death proved to be a spiritual catastrophe. His reform, however exhilarating and sincere it might have been, ended a failure. Huldah had doubtless sensed this and had tried to prevent it by her prediction, but in vain.

At the Beginning of a True Biblical Renewal

Thanks to the discovery of a scroll of Torah, Huldah's name remains linked with Scripture. Today we think that the text discovered in the Temple was probably an early version of Deuteronomy, perhaps just the section on the "two ways." This hypothesis is attractive, for how could they fail being struck on discovering such an appeal in the midst of the purification of the Temple? "See, I am setting before you today a blessing and a curse: the blessing, if you obey the commandments of the Lord your God that I am commanding you today; and the curse, if you do not obey the commandments of the Lord your God, but turn from the way that I am commanding you today, to follow other gods that you have not known" (Deut 11:26–28). The scroll must not have been very long since Shaphan reads it to the king, and then Josiah reads the whole text to the assembled people (2 Kgs 22:10; 23:2).

The discovery and then the authentication and interpretation of the book by Huldah provoke a veritable biblical renewal. In solemn fashion Josiah puts the word of God back into the center of Jewish life. Under the impulse of Huldah, of prophets, priests, and king, the people join in a new covenant with God. Torah becomes the "book of the covenant" (23:1–3).

By giving the words and threats of the book that had been found the weight of divine words, Huldah encourages King Josiah both to implement his religious reform and to try to ward off the misfortunes of the people as they rebuild their unity. In order to show the new way clearly, once all traces of pagan ways were eradicated, the celebration of Passover in the Jerusalem Temple was restored. No longer would it take place in the local sanctuaries as used to be done (23:21–23). We are present at an important movement toward the centralization of the cult.

While Josiah's reform was short-lived, the Book of the Covenant still is alive and current with its fundamental message of one God, one people, one Torah.

One God

The affirmation that there is no other god than the "God of Abraham, of Isaac, and of Jacob," the God of the matriarchs and the patriarchs, is at the heart of the Jewish faith. That can be understood in at least two ways.

First it can mean that this is the God of Israel, and the other peoples of the world each have their own god. This can be called "monolatry," with its implication: respect for the gods and the cultural values of every people.

But the idea of one God can also be understood in a universal sense. God is one, one for Israel and for all humanity. We call this interpretation monotheism (Deut 4:39; Mark 12:29–32; Luke 20:38). Islam has pretty much the same idea: "In the name of God, the gracious and merciful, say: God is one, the impenetrable; he begets not, and neither is he begotten, and there is none equal to him" (Qur'an 112).

In this understanding the affirmation that God is one has the corollary of rejecting every form of idolatry and every alien religious custom. Syncretism, which was still flourishing at the beginning of Josiah's reign, would have no place in the realm of God, "the master of heaven and earth."

One People

This one God, at once entirely other and very near, has chosen a people to be companions in living a particular history. That seems to be God's freedom, to choose one or another creature, or a whole people, with whom to engage in the adventure of a unique friendship, although not necessarily to the exclusion of all the others.

In this context, it is important not to see this choice as favoritism, but to discern its meaning instead. The theme of election in Israel has always been a delicate subject by reason of its history. For in choosing a people without a particular prerogative other than having accepted his proposal of partnership, God shows the height, the breadth, and the depth of the divine love, while at the same time showing something about the process of divine revelation.

Always noting the defects of the chosen people—the threats against Josiah are an example of this—God is revealed as "a God merciful and gracious, slow to anger, and abounding in steadfast love" (Exod 34:6). They can always return to God and undertake a reform. They can always return to this God in search of humans, to this God who, even before election, asks: "Where are you?" (Gen 3:9).

Through the particularism of his relationship with the Jewish people, God tells us that history is possible only if we recognize that we are fallible, humble, and free enough ceaselessly to make the journey of return. In returning to God, in reclaiming our place in the partnership plan, we find again our rightful place and responsibilities in society.

God and Israel: one history that finds its true worth in solidarity, in opening up to the nations. This is a constant challenge and yields its fruits only in reciprocity.

One Torah

The discovery of the scroll of the Law and the visit to the prophet Huldah bring the king and people back to the demands of Torah. In the Decalogue given to Moses on Sinai, God is revealed as a liberating God. The One who has delivered the Hebrews from the violence of Pharaoh wants them to become liberators in their turn. Escaping from Egypt is neither forgetting nor negating the experience of Egypt, but rather going beyond it. It is a clear demonstration of how life in society is possible without recourse to violence, and that the economy as well as the state can be founded on a sound ethical basis.

It is probably this conception of the world and of life provided by Torah that lets Huldah foretell a peaceful end for King Josiah. As she encourages him in his reform, she lets him know that the reform necessarily implies placing his confidence in God alone and renouncing useless wars.

This was a revolutionary message in this time of conquest when only violence assured power. It is a difficult path to follow, even for Josiah the reformer. Later on, fired with enthusiasm, he will prefer war to diplomacy: Huldah's warning was ineffective after all. There is only one way, a single and exclusive way, but all the same we are free to choose between "life and prosperity," and "death and adversity" (Deut 30:15).

Prophet at a Turning Point in History

In spite of its sad end, the reign of Josiah marks a considerable turning point. In the prophetic and literary movements that characterize the years of his reign, what really was Huldah's role? We need no other response to this question than the two gates of the Temple to which, according to tradition, she gave her name and which reflect, as in a mirror, the two tables of the Law.

Epilogue

Three Women of Hope

THE LIVES OF MIRIAM the nomad, Hannah the visionary, and Huldah the townswoman show us that the function of a prophet is registered in the usual concept of time as made up of past, present, and future.

By Attachment to Tradition

The past refers to tradition. The prophetic message of our three heroes is part of the message of a long chain of women and men who have made history. It takes account of the essential and existential values proper to the people while at the same time integrating new values, in the case of Miriam, Hannah, and Huldah the values taught them by their experiences as women. As they lean on the word of God, they open new channels.

The disobedience of Miriam and the midwives is in no way an egotistical act. These women risk their lives to give the Hebrews a future. Their gesture is inspired by the promise made before to Abraham and Sarah that they would have numerous progeny.

When Hannah in her suffering finds the boldness to connect her barrenness with that of her era, she is anticipating and announcing the Talmudic sages who will write centuries later: "Three keys are in the hands of the Holy One, blessed be he, which he entrusts to no messenger: the key that commands and opens the womb, the key that commands and opens the clouds of rain, and the key that commands resurrection." Hannah's rebellion is her response to God's desire to make every human being, even woman, in the divine image and likeness. By standing up, Hannah revives a hope in herself and in the people; judgment belongs to God and not to human beings.

As for Huldah, she depicts feminine rigor and severity. Without retreating from God's judgment on the kings of Judah, she tries to introduce the idea that word and act should be identical. Studying Torah and putting it into practice are inseparably intertwined. This is why in a culture where violence presides, it took her sort of courage to suggest negotiation and diplomacy to resolve conflicts.

Always with Values of the Present

Without the constant help of the present, without an adaptation to the reality of the present, however rich a people's values might be, they remain sterile.

Like all the prophets Miriam, Hannah, and Huldah were immersed in the events of their times. To discern the meaning hidden to ordinary mortals, they linked historical circumstances with personal situations. In doing so, they not only put history back on track, but also reoriented it, resituated it in the mainstream of Torah.

For them human situations have to be compared. In this way tradition finds its meaning and becomes a source of inspiration for the present. The dialogue between ethics and engagement in history is one of the basic givens of life for these three prophets. This is how they do their work.

And Preparing the Future

Linking the future with prophecy seems commonplace. But in making this connection we are not thinking about predicting a future event. Rather it is a matter of the capacity to anticipate which values are susceptible of future development.

In this relation between what is present and what will happen later, the future is not the expression of a roving imagination or a utopian dream, but the clear perception of what is, and what is realizable. As we have been able to see with these three prophets, this subtle discernment has to be actualized in the implementation of a strategy that fosters the emergence of a scenario that is deemed possible but not necessarily probable. When she chooses Pharaoh's daughter for the adoptive mother of Moses, Miriam gives us the example of a strategy that offers the maximum chance for the survival and future of her brother.

Conscious of the indispensable intertwining of linear history with the will of God, Miriam, Hannah, and Huldah display a refined art in their capacity to link flexibility and firmness. They know by experience that if history is made by women and men, it is continually susceptible to the disrupting inrushes of God, and also continually dependent on divine grace. God and the human being are committed to each other.

A Creative Limit

Prophecy, like that practiced by our three heroes, can be summed up in the refusal of human alienation in all its forms. When history comes off the rails, when the human race is bullied, someone has to call a halt. This is never easy to do and often even more difficult to maintain.

In a chaotic context often marked by violence, we have seen Miriam, Hannah, and Huldah stand up and say no. Setting a limit in patriarchal society is no easy thing for a woman to do. Ridicule did not spare Hannah, and Huldah was chosen because they thought her incapable of a harsh judgment. The skill these women displayed consists in declaring a limit that does not so much exclude as become creative.

Whether in saving baby boys, or retrieving the dignity of woman, or even upholding a difficult reform, the imagination that they showed leaves us astonished. Not a single limit that did not become a channel to the future!

Today we hear that our time lacks prophetic voices, female or male. Could it be that prophecy is currently expressed more by groups of people who organize together to say no? Are not the women of the Plaza de Majo in Argentina the direct descendants of Miriam and the midwives? And how could we not discern the prophetic bearing of the peace and democracy movements of the Middle East, of humanitarian organizations of solidarity, of women's liberation movements, or the Truth and Reconciliation Commission in South Africa?

Prophecy and Liberation

Yes, thanks to Miriam, Hannah, and Huldah, prophecy has been feminized, without losing any of its revolutionary character, which has also opened the door to its democratization. Vindicating their inalienable right to word and act, these three women have placed their prophetic engagement alongside creative protest in that free space where struggle is changed into the promise of a future.

Miriam, Hannah, and Huldah had the audacity and intuitive good sense to place their personal situations on the same level as the moral problems of their times. Their prophetic engagement, rooted in a mystical vision of the person and history, gives the problem of evil both an individual and a cosmic dimension. Indeed, each of these women's adventures is limited enough to allow her to get to the heart of her experience and broad enough to be situated from the outset on the scale of universal values.

In this perspective, prophecy and life are united in a single liberating hope.